Ismene's Survivable Resistance

By the same author:

Ismene's Survivable Resistance

Claire Gaskin

PUNCHER & WATTMANN

First published in 2021
Published by Puncher and Wattmann
PO Box 279
Waratah NSW 2298

http://www.puncherandwattmann.com
puncherandwattmann@bigpond.com

NATIONAL
LIBRARY
OF AUSTRALIA

A catalogue record for this book is available from the National Library of Australia

ISBN   9781922571038

Cover design by Miranda Douglas

Printed by Lightning Source International

In this collection of poetry I adopt Ismene's name, from Sophocles play Antigone, to explore what survivable resistance may look like. I am shedding some light on what it is like to live on after Greek-tragedy-like trauma is over. I am suggesting that Antigone's sister Ismene had an alternative way of resisting abusers of power and of living on her own terms. These poems are written in the voice of a contemporary Ismene.

Ismene's thirsts

in this binary library
a murder of fictions
crows gather in corners
it is work to witness
question marks
polished apples

one side limp
I called an ambulance
this memory smells nutty
the first line I trusted

hot under a tree in the outback
a bag of lychees
declarations of love are not love

front teeth crack the husk
translucence of trace

the bee on my chest witnesses the space between beats
I dusted my brother's body
the dandelions nod affirmation
the butterfly heavy with the want does not land

the day I went to get results
my notebook opened an incision
lay lined
an inky river

the little boy runs into
my failure of ground
there is a beach where the two rivers meet
the Jamieson, the Goulburn

not remembering protected them from the birds, their crimes

a woman on a horse tells us one river is warmer, one faster

standing in water two arms end in a heart

their crimes fell like coins out of holes in the lining
yellow leaves are boats moving as fast as the colluding current

I have to stay till I arrive
medicated into the seams
two elbows on the table
the wood smells like old books
my notebook spread flightless

a muddy pond of tea cools in my hands
sitting in the wind of hospital corridors

cockatoos rip apart the morning
the river swallows the fall
my mother raised her arms in prayer to the clothes line

blood flows from the left atrium to the right
flies land on my denial
the privacy of grief

she took her two hands off her walker
onto my shoulders
pegged me with prayer

the two rivers don't meet
the Jamieson ends in the Goulburn

constancy

my compliance cannot be bought
I can rest out of sight but not in focus
visible from space
the glass bottom boat has a stable relationship with the moving view
maybe my depression means my mother bored me even when dying
like my dog yawning when she cannot incorporate what is enacted
before her
the largest living thing
I dream my mother smaller than when alive
my lack of commitment, resistance to presence
I am not in pain, I am in disguise
I had to check the baby was still alive
he uses language like
you bought it on yourself
then says it is not mass bleaching
somewhere under the stone
of anxiety to please
is the beauty of the closed door
the silver teapot covered in algae
he asks me to make him tea
the more I clean the more it needs cleaning
I use a small bristled brush to clean the spout
it is full of cockroaches
they scatter as I flick them away
even as more take their place

breath

the seagull is one shade slower than the ceiling fan
the heart one beat lighter than the clouded sky

akin to surrender but distinct from defeat
the active state of rest

he gave to take away

as I come into focus I came into anger

the bone on bone of marginalia
where thought meets movement

the shared history of rocks warming in the sun

when she put her key in the lock
it remembered her
because she had rented her body to breath

present at an event

what witness is pulled down with the blinds
shot through with moth holes of light
positivity can kill you
hands   ice fists

shot through with moth holes of light
I saw the season change on fact
my hands frozen syllables
a cyclone and a tear in my soup

I saw the season change on fact
there is no floor
a frozen tear and a cyclone in my soup
sums in my mother's hand

there is no floor
falls off the table
the paper with sums in my mother's hand
I can't find

it falls off the table
I saw autumn leaves caught in a hair net
I can't find
a heartbeat comma in the glasses case

I saw autumn leaves caught in a hair net
on the asphalt outside the restaurant
a heartbeat comma in the glasses case
of the long intake of relief grief

on the asphalt outside the restaurant
the glass grapes and shrinking lemons
of the long intake of grief relief
the facts like scraps of medical journals

the glass grapes and shrinking lemons
swept under the chesterfields you sit on of symptoms you don't have
the facts like scraps of medical journals
now there is new research to witness against loss

swept under the chesterfields you sit on of symptoms you don't have
syllables can kill you
now there is new research to witness against loss
what is pulled down with the blinds

brothers

in the sunny backyard
the blood from plums running down his forearms
he fed the dog lifesavers as he smoked
in the bungalow he shared with Eteocles
he painted the room purple and lacquered
a huge poster of a racing car to the wall

if you boys want to fight go outside Creon would say
my brothers fought under the apple tree
I watched my aunty clean pasta sauce off the wall

there was witness in his eyes

Antigone would say don't provoke Polynices

words form and fail at the point of touch

I dreamt my mother covered the body with a sheet   said it was time

I have no love for a friend who loves in words alone

swatting the buzz of childhood away from my ear
I didn't know what advice to give Antigone

the plaster contracts
the tap drips
in every house I have found myself empty in

Eteocles used to rock in his sleep

I have finished cobwebbing the house
the dead accumulate on the doorstep

my love for my sister
dangerous black water you do not know the depth of

Polynices would add knots to the leather band tied around his wrist
Antigone talked of his lower lip quivering
said he had a soft heart
he was expelled from five schools

looking out at the flat lining of the bay
the sky rips at the seams

Eteocles with an orange paper crown on his head
told bad jokes at Christmas dinner
loudly claimed authority on every subject

Polynices was the paperboy who bought the newsagency
bought and sold bought and sold
we started to have things at home when Polynices started to 'work'
like crates of wine and billiard tables

fat drops of rain resound in my pond of tea
the elm shatters gold and red
into the begging bowl of my lap

Eteocles played the xylophone
had a job as a wedding singer
failed matriculation five times

I am starting to have moments of feeling like it never happened
there is a before and there is an after
I am sewing them together
in the seams is the sea green of me

I see my colleague
as I stand at *house of cards* for coffee
it is drizzling
she is on the other side of the zebra crossing
I call
she is wearing leopard skin to the union meeting
Antigone wore leopard skin to the funerals

Eteocles struggled with his weight
on a run with him when I was bent over double
he urged me
always focus on something in the near distance

I raise my hand in the meeting

I don't deny a thing

I never agreed with Antigone that we were rooted in the shame of our famil
I said it she lived it
Polynices slept with a knife under his pillow
a comforter to smooth against his cheek

my sister is on the couch

her knees drawn up to her chest
a blanket over her head
rocking
chanting
the truth is in the pudding
there are fairy dresses for the school concert
in piles of red and gold tulle on every surface
he is at the kitchen table
his head on his arms
I know not to go near him

the heavy lidded language

words witness words
stepping after
step into the clearing
a sentence unfurls
ends in a stop

the stopping is a window
into the womb
rushing throat

language is the house not the home

the bringing of eyelids down over the listening

the virginity of humility

two hands come together in front of the heart's
hole that never closed at birth
bringing this to this

the moments like stones on the path
the space between ideas

the evidence of prayer

Ismene

the dictionary of dead flowers
tells me I am essential but dispensable

there will always be a space for you she is saying

the weight of an old cat on my lap

untied from the mast
salt in my joints
I'm not in The Odyssey
I author myself

peopled to this place this couch
face to face with the page

the weight of an old betrayal
a room inside my dreams I didn't know was there
unsheathed splintered claws

walled in her word there was no room for me
the ceiling fan blades in my teaspoon

glass

the grey aches at the heart of shame
in the heart of the statue

the blood pulls both ways
pools deepcentre

hushing on the shore
rising

she didn't give up beginnings for becoming

bringing the horizons together
closing the curtains
to the held vase of a throat

poetry as presence

words rise to the surface fall back into salt sea

the space between knowing and not

the lemon tree rests its lemons on the shed roof

just to close my eyes brings together
my heart wearing out my body

the drawer spills
birds of blame
my hands spill
cross hatched early life
a dark spot on the reading of my palm

peeling back layers of need
to the inner thigh of desire

it does not describe
it inhales
it holds its breath to listen

Ismene in a Twelve Step Programme

I can tell you about powerlessness
step one
knowing it is going to happen and being able to do nothing
Antigone chooses to die rather than survive abuse
pinned down his sweat dripping in my face
saying you may as well enjoy it
something severed it
wasn't love and sex it was abuse from love
he didn't love me
all my abusers before that had loved me
I dreamt I was walking through the rubble of my family home
seeking shelter there
I loved them that is what children do
consequences of knowing things I could not believe
I had sex again with him to make him feel
I could have learnt
not spent a life trying to make my abusers love me
if I'd been able to be present
my boyfriend's parting words it's not the same
he came back thirty-three years later
said he could have dealt with it better
believing it I knew it was not true
sitting on the steps of ourselves
cleaning my feet
constantly re-traumatising each other
I did my best not to survive it
meet and repeat the annihilation in addiction
I am here because I know about a life time of refusal
I dreamt I was painting

I wasn't in control of my medium and I had the wrong brushes
you don't have to believe to pray
survival is the radical act
wasn't I reason enough for her to stay alive
what is survivable resistance
Polynices was already dead
I know the Greek Tragedy thing once it is set in motion it
must play out
but I'm still here to feel the sun on my body and the water to
witness my blaring heart
my abuser was giving me admission
something my family could never give me
I have to grip the arms of my chair to stay present
I use sex to avoid intimacy
did she love Polynices more than life
is that love
she made him her god
I get that she felt like he was irreplaceable
what was I
but so was she
sister
I could bury my dead in private
she needed it to be seen by other
is to survive it to comply
she died to what they call sanity logic law so I could live
she covered up that the first burial was mine
I couldn't stay in the house with Creon
I took off
got as far as Sydney before I met someone
we swam drank had lots of sex moved on to the next beach
whenever we wanted
a job at a magazine the editor had sent everyone out
lying on a hot rock by black water

the sound of metal bowls being placed on the ground
I am left I am what is left
my body a bargain with presence
where things move in the breeze
it was the gaze of the train
the inevitability
the lake hollows the sound of voices

tension

standing waiting at the lights
like a picked daisy
between thumb and forefinger
a house of thrumming bees
my mother sways
low blood pressure
of on-my-knees in shifting sands
of your push me pull me
draw a curved line in the sugar
tides of coffee
where trucks use their air brakes
a cup meets a saucer
birds stitch to seamless night
there is glass between
surrender and extinction
steep staircases of railway stations
and libraries of rising histories
blame restrained
tears of rage break my resistance to receive
in the circle of listening the centre is held

the body lesson

syllables of understanding hit the ground
in an utterance
stilled by the sun
the dream of wanting to enter water
a candle in front of a mirror is a watched lake
what will happen next
rest requires less
inhabiting the smooth surfaces of self
breath hollows out the body as the sea hollows out a shell
perpetually spiralling witness
I miss my sister's sharp clarity
who are we when the time comes
I listen to the house contract
the day snares on four o'clock

same purr

different cat lands on the bed
same abandonment different person
here in a room full of my mother's death and a vase of water
Antigone's death doesn't bother me as much as her being confined in a cave
don't move they say as I go into the tunnel
if a group of crows is a murder
what is a conference of cardiologists
when the hole is closed will I still write poetry
maybe I'll do paperwork better
six petals radiate five flowers of commitment
yellow stamen heart
I say to my cowering mother
you have the right to make yourself safe
story is the blood seeping through the bandage over her eyes not Oedipus'

horizon

we unmade the bed as we
lay in it touch by touch
unthreading fingers
the lead sinker
overboard
lost on the same page
underlined in her
unspoken gaze

tilted

I sister the chair across the cafe table
it's a cup full of tannin shade
weighing down that end of the sea-saw
it's blue the sky, the ocean behind me
its breeze loosening dark corners
the pen moving across the page clearing dream

what words

are stiffening my neck
have thinned artery walls

it's not unusual to be made redundant to self
caught in the blankets witnessing
the candle flame flinches

a sparrow flying at the window
a stone in the hand the colour of crime

Ismene reads her psych's book on dissociation

the mattress holds the heat of the mind haunted
the dream-rivers reason with the tree roots to remember
the cradle flinches in the breeze fracturing
holding through the night of nights de-realized
this journey does not involve going anywhere fragmented
my mind outside my body having a body is to blame

pulling the rip cord of silk self-blame
not present feels like I am ghosting haunting
my skin alight with the pain of a refrain fragment
blood to forgiveness throbbing in my knuckles remembered
narratives run through my fingers de-realized
time calculated in the imprint of my face as the clay fractures

the stone dropped into the pool of my pelvis fracturing
I forgive you father for you have sinned and are to blame
the glass of water on the window sill reacting to the foundations
        de-realized
I am matter I do matter I am a spirit haunted
thrown into the sea of ancestors remembered
my feet are rubbed out as the waves fragment

the ticking of the passing bike in winking time fragments
I see the effect but not the cause fracturing
the floors worn through in a puddle of raw wood to remember
my hands mangled birds the weather blames
you cannot perceive the imperceptible through perception but
        meaning is a haunting
awareness is one thing action is another substituting is

depersonalisation

disintegration of identity experience de-realized
how traumatised people talk in sentence fragments
a demolished base is not a safe haunt
scenes flash topic switching and my credibility fractures
the two major tasks in life are to love and to work not to be blamed
the more severe the less remembered

I fight through the curtains to get into my psych's room to remember
the smell in the dark of my mother's wardrobe their bedroom
      depersonalised
it's harder to be autonomous when the culpable don't take the blame
in murky water hair in waving reeds submerged trees and
      bone fragments
on the surface of the lake the clouds fracture
wanting it to be other than it is doesn't stop the truth haunting

a poem is re-membering in collaged fragments
limits de-realised from forming fatigue fractures
a child with no outline feels to blame it is an oceanic haunting

Ismene in a boxing writing workshop

(inspired by Donna Lyon's Left, Write, Hook Boxing and Writing
Workshops for survivors of sexual abuse and trauma)

jab, jab, cross, hook, cross
under the drag of the crowd
jab, jab, cross, hook, cross, hook, cross
down on bent knees
down on bloodied knees
down on pleasing knees as the mozzies bite me
the fern garden like the dank of the wardrobe
jab, jab, cross, hook, cross, hook, cross, duck, cross, duck, cross
the cowering left barbed wire fence broken bottles
stuck in the lift surrounding body sounds
jab, cross, hook, cross, upper, upper
muscle around memory
jab, cross, hook, cross, upper, upper, hook, cross
I remember I kicked Antigone's boyfriends
as soon as they walked in the door
where does a seven-year-old get that from
they were bent over double
I was swift   accurate
use the iron bar
hit the bag
vocalise
go hard
I want my life back
isolated on the page I have made a life
jab, cross, hook, cross, upper, upper, hook, cross, hook, cross
I keep dreaming Antigone is not dead
I have been making it up   being hyperbolic
jab, cross, hook, cross, upper, upper x5, 10 shuffles

the pen making contact
a page sweating
a translucent stone   murky eye   keyhole
bloody knuckles   braised with pain
a life of self-blame
the gloves the face the mask
the bag of body
plank rotations
shaky hands secreted by mind
body secrets whispered crevices
I'm in my body I feel it now
coming out of the dentist   face half numb
this is how it feels to get smacked in the face
I didn't feel it at the time   I feel it now
this is how it feels to get smacked in the face
jab, jab, cross, hook, cross x 10, squat jump x 5
the kiss of fist to bag
under the unbroken surface reflecting sky
drowned bodies
secrets excreted
a trail of red petals
I am fire married to flight
on my knees beside altars
the cold smell of marble
I rubbed off the writing on the wall
I wasn't to blame but I am accountable
broke the back of promise to self-annihilate
fists swimming
a weighted blanket over me
hard to forgive what I haven't been given
dream of going into surgery trying to spit out the drugs
chanting and dogma
proof in sensory

oven warmed blanket
detail specific
case studies of the heart
beaten humanity
weather eaten words drop like contact
the throat between rocks that the river moves through
being believed is being in becoming
what does it mean to arrive at wellness
crying tears of teeth

I invite you

we plant promises in the full force of the depth of us

alliteration draws the words through the eye of the needle

the point guided with eye contact

mending the hole in the folding fabric of free fall

in my father's house are many mansions

a fox slipped away across moonlit railway lines
like wakefulness from sleep

I dreamt I was living in a burning mansion

I don't want to be fixed I want to be compensated
for while I see the holes in listening
night birds make

the witness makes it happen
my sister sits in the shallows of dreams' deep time

the rope through the holes in the rock of what is not
remembered

the page is a wall of sensory deprivation
the words dredge luggage and laughter

I loved the people who held me captive

rain and cupboards spewing mud
my bathroom full of dragonflies

alone with my ghosts

with every hinge aching in the wind
my blood thinned

in the womb of the car
she saying you won't have to worry about me anymore

known hunger is permanent

my heart undermined
the flesh grown over metal

my bed unmade the weight of me
a launching not resting place

I walked sentences in the sand

the page is a net that dredges nightmare

the wind lifts the labels off forgiveness
the water resents
soothes the inside of a shell
I curl up in, as a fleshy mass
the pain in making small
in the back seat of the car
as she drove erratically

Ismene after the Royal Commission

the truth is I went back
to the ruins of the house
I paid with my being to live in

the gate like an opening and closing in the heart

my dead mother still living in the one room not burnt out

the floor forever giving

someone swallowed a mouthful of her dressmaking pins

you have a persecution complex she would say

now *they* stand accused
I watched it burn

my history wearing a meaning mask

don't cause conflict she would say

I couldn't save my mother

my heart is not banging in the walls
it is the the wall of words I push through
realising it's a bead curtain

you are over sensitive

I go to say something and …
there is a vacuum
there is an empty space at the table for me

I couldn't save my sister

forgetting is a stone

the only place she looks alive is in my dreams

the pretending was so profound it became forecasting

all that is left of the window is the brown crucifix of a wooden frame

the floor tilting towards the viewer

emptied of arrival

there are three wooden chairs summoning resurrection

Ismene's Patent Foramen Ovale closure

was I just a plot device in Antigone's story
a disposable body at a crime scene
her shadow still on me
a gatekeeper in dreams

a disposable body in a crime scene
the fourth wall dismantled
gatekeepers dream
separating like oil and water

the fourth wall dismantled
the child in the photo looking out from engagement and enquiry
mind and body separating like oil and water
smiling at the photographer

the child in the photograph looking out of engagement and
enquiry
standing room in the heart only
I was thinking the best of the photographer
underneath it all emptied of story

standing room in the heart only
I put you away in a tabernacle
underneath it all emptied of story
I sit till the sediment settles

I put you away in the tabernacle heart
pinning myself to the page with every word written
I sit till the sediment settles
like skinning an unconscious mouse

pinning its skin back with every word written
revealing its chest to see it beat
skinning an unconscious mouse
I wake feeling I have been running

I opened its chest to see its heart beat
when I'm pinned madness feels like freedom
I wake feeling like I have been running all night
don't fall in love with the messenger

pinned madness is freedom
he said I'm happy if I've fixed your migraines as well
don't fall in love with the messenger
I didn't say I'm glad my body was of service in your story

my cardiologist said if I've fixed you I'm happy
in the ultrasound I saw the four chambers
I didn't say I've advocated for this for four years of specialists on chesterfields
I saw the wall thickened where the metal device is in place

the four chambers of my heart a flap waving in the flow
her shadow still on me
the wall thickened with the metal device in place
no longer a plot device robbed of story

buried

the familiar grave grit in my eyes
a forgotten unbroken roar of ocean under skin
betrayal caught in the blades of the ceiling fan
I open the curtains to the forgiving page
the storm in a cradle
the flickering leaves aflame
the bed porous
I remake movement every morning
poured into the shape of a shelter
from shame
a cup of hands
I cannot remember without a swallow
solitude a cool glass of water
unkinking the hose
after too many coffees
watering plants bathed in light
she got too close to the dying enquiry
it reignited
her throat caught fire breathing the text
a cup of water poured over the drain and constricted larynx
nobody listened to the content of my mother's complaint
I did but she didn't see me
the rain came down with the words

Ismene goes to a 70th birthday

I am a survivor of a bullet hovering at my temple; I thought I saw
it aimed between my eyes when a puppy came to sit on my lap; I
thought I'd had an intuition; but Antigone said look to your left;
and there it was sitting just out of my peripheral vision; nothing
you can do she said and the Antigones standing around her and
behind her assented; it is set to go off; you won't know when but
it will go off; I could catch it in my hand but when I let it go it
would resume its position beside my temple; I decided I would
sit on the step in the sun and meditate so I would be at peace
when it fired; there was a flat red cushion covered in garden
grit on a step above; others had gone before me; I dusted it off;
placed the cushion on the step now in the sun; made myself
comfortable; I heard singing; other survivors were at the party;
I hadn't know they were there; I tentatively asked them what
they thought if I nailed the bullet down; it was spongy like an
ear plug; or would that set it off; they told me of other survivors
and what they had done; some of the stories were tragic; one
had dodged the bullet somehow but it had hit and killed a
bystander; I resolved I would take the bullet; some scientifically
gifted clear thinking party conversationalists stepped forward;
said there may be a way to change the trajectory and began
working on it in earnest in the shed with physics and wire; it
wasn't that they may succeed that mattered to me but that a
whole different believing existed

mother of mercy

she looks down and inward at her poetry because there is no one above her
she is not an intermediary
she is not inside not outside but sheltered
it is her survivable resistance
not either side but in-between

the action of making secrets self-know

I don't tonight don't to with be alone want to disclosure
want to be I tonight don't disclosure to to my with alone want to
alone with my don't tonight with disclosure want be to alone want my I be
disclosure my I tonight don't disclosure want with alone be to
tonight disclosure my tonight with I alone want don't
I don't want to be alone with my disclosure tonight

the essence of repression lies simply in turning something away, and keeping it at a distance, from the conscious
— Freud

I remember lying in bed in terror
I remember him walking quietly around the house at night
the broken strap of his scandal hitting the floor every second footfall
I don't remember what happened once I went to sleep
I remember hearing breathing behind the door
I remember watching people in robes chanting on television
I remember we did not have a television
I remember them watching a horror movie
I remember we did not have a television
I remember her guarding the door
I remember me under the sheet laughing
I remember seeing the bed from above
I don't remember what happened under the sheets
I remember to tell every subsequent lover don't touch me when I am asleep
I won't remember it's you I remember to tell them
I remember not to go to sleep

Ismene gardening

I have to lose sight of the loss of life
we finish gardening at eight o'clock

installed with self
the sun on the side of my face

the ache in the softest wash of wisdom
this is why we wordlessly snail across pages

my pillow fatigued
the loaves of bread that sleep muttering prayers

the elbow of dark water dream smells of fuel

I am tired of prowling cats
the light on the page like his gaze on me
my hair gets so matted from being with him
what do I want to contribute to saying
this adding and subtracting
the love of his laugh
we are carer or we are cured which one do we choose
we both wake hyper-vigilant

closing the opening with doors

are you growing or are you growing the void

forgiving your forgetting

gathering the flags and scarves tied to the fence around self

I was buried in a bedroom looking at a bookcase
a hall of mirrors a hall of family photos

stay away from him when he is full of flight

the lake of light on my watch face
the clock in the classroom was going backwards
I went backwards towards my mothergrandmother
the rattling of the gate against the latch

who gets caught in the net of words

the clouded window the see-through body
no more trying to please the unpleasable

light wipes the slate clean
the lake of light on my watch face means I can't see his hands

it just takes one poem to believe you

I wear my body out like a rubber glove

I feel the tick of the clock under my armpits

write a poem about sparrows in cafes

Ismene dreams

a cathedral of people dancing salsa around the petrol bourses

the play made of my early life is called *Antigone*, not *Sisters* look it up

I dreamt I was bleeding great clots of blood
I couldn't find a toilet
I found a foul outdoor drop dunny full of flies
I decided I would just sit over it and bleed

I dreamt I was in bed with someone
in a falling down mansion
we were barged in on by debt collectors

I dreamt I had a friend's family photos
they were landscapes
he wasn't necessarily happy I had them
they were photos celebrating his long-term relationship

I dreamt I was wearing slippers in the snow

I start where the pen hits the page
the long note of the horizon
where the sea is a fold line in the sky
same pain different wave
days that stretch and expand in the sun
the sonata like a shawl of breeze over my shoulders

Ismene reading *The Betrayal Bond* (Patrick J. Carnes)

Person 1
Promise
Do and think and believe as I say and I will love you
not just own you and use you.
True agenda or intent
control never loved me

Person 2
Promise
Be responsible for all my feelings and everything will be okay
and I won't commit suicide
and I will approve of you
and be proud and keep you safe and care for you.
True agenda and intent
she knew everything was never going to be okay
and she never gave approval or safety
she did not care for me and did not keep me safe
her intent was to have her emotional needs met

Person 3
Promise
Do as I say and provide for all my impossible needs,
cure my abandonment issues
and I won't terrorize you and the people around you.
True agenda and intent
control and destruction

Person 4
Same as above

Person 5
Same as above

Person 6
Promise
Work hard do unpaid work and you will be rewarded.
True intent
serve the status of the sandstone

Person 7
Promise
Do as I say and provide for all my needs and please me and I won't leave yc
and I'll provide for your emotional needs and be supportive.
We will heal together.
Be everything she could not be and I won't treat you as I treat her.
Intent
breaking up with me every time I thought for myself
exploiting my abandonment issues
leaving me when at my most vulnerable

Person 8
Promise
Be exclusively mine and I will love you.
Intent
control

Person 9
Promise
Answer all my needs and I will love you.
You are special.

I can only talk to you, only you understand.
Intent
having all her needs met
she always abandoned me when a better offer came up

Person 10
As above

Conclusion
I will always abandon myself when a better and difficult offer comes up

Ismene teaches creative writing for thirty years

I keep writing because I have to. I write when it's too intense to contain. So it can exist outside of me. So I can read it as if it is a poem. I keep writing because I was robbed of my sense of being. Others were also robbed of it. I keep writing myself into existence. I keep writing and teaching because life depends on being relational and I was robbed of that. Reality was ripped from me. I was told what was happening wasn't happening so I had no relationship with shared reality. Writing and teaching is shared reality. As a child I didn't have a shared reality, my private and public world had no relationship. I was completely isolated. What was going on in my inner world, my home, had no relationship with the general consensus of what family should be. This is what living a lie is for families like mine that institutionalise and ritualise the abuse of children. For families that abuse children then go to work the next day as upstanding citizens. This living a lie is programming of survivors to live a double life. To live is to breathe in and out. Living is shaped in the shared space between the breaths, between reader and writer, between teacher and teaching. Without these exchanges there is no life. For there to be life there needs to be exchange. Breathing brings my inner and outer world into relationship, so does being writer and being reader. I keep writing breath. Writing is breathing out, reading is breathing in. As soon as I write and then read it, I have created a reader, a self as reader. My reading self proves my writing self exists. I have created a relationship between my writing self and my reading self. I have created a relationship with self. There needs to be relationship for there to be a sense of being in living relationship with living. The relationship is living. I have created a sense of a living self. The space between reader and writer keeps shifting and shaping my becoming. I write because to write is survivable resistance against erasure. I don't take it to court; I leave that to other fighting survivors. I've been in court with my sister. I know what it's like. I fight; I take it to a public of my own making. I write myself into the shape of a person.

not another fucking sunset

blue towel
three friends and sand
a peach heart dripping into the bay
what does it make you feel he says
loss I say
how do you feel I ask him
I am worried it's not going to rise again
it will rise again
I know it will rise again I just don't know if I will be alive to see it
I want to hold it up
how do you feel, I ask her
I like it it gives me hope the night is my time
it'll be midday there he says
the underbelly of the clouds a rose pink
then a deeper bruised blush
and a chill on the skin
the breeze a beginning of forgiving
she leaves she is wet and cold
the sand the sitting the incoming the outgoing
of breath of water smoothing sand
the foam the deepening solitude
the breathing the holding edge
the sun extinguished the red wine stains
the bottom of the green glass
the bottle finished
the shape the support of the shifting
nothing stays forever he says
three friends shot in three weeks
the fires the survivors the stories

rising to our feet
we walk up the steep sandy steps

Ismene loves

to love is to truly have survived

she has her head bowed
and her palms are open
but she is standing on a serpent
a serpent that wraps the world

she has subdued it

I know why you drink

I drank a bottle of scotch a day after I was raped
and my boyfriend left me

you drink to celebrate life
but you get drunk to annihilate it

I'm standing on my serpent
my head is bowed and my palms are open
it writhes beneath my feet

I pray to her who has subdued
to step into her
with my head bowed and my palms open

I know why you drink

my ex-husband quoted
first you take a drink

then the drink takes you

now he says
I'm not going to drink anymore
and I'm not going to drink any less

the irony is that's the humour
I love for him

I know there is and has been your wars
I know what you drink for

my wars go on behind closed doors
against women and children
in the halls and kitchens of honoured institutions

behind closed lids
where the serpent rears its head
and wraps around my dreams
where the memories mercury

mercurial

Mother of Mercy

for he does apparently exist

he does exist, do I exist
the chair moves into place
there are santas on the tablecloth
and wind in the trees
he does exist he can be searched
I thought I made him up
he who spent a whole family christmas
randomly bringing up *false memory syndrome*
he is my brother, my mother bore him
for he does apparently exist
because of the charges laid against him
I thought he couldn't work with children anymore
he is affiliated with a primary school
he has a PhD supervised by a bishop
he publishes articles, advises curriculums
he writes transphobic articles
what is not searchable are the charges
so he does apparently exist
he has seven children
two small boys he sent back on the plane
with the priest after my mother's funeral
gory be to god
he does apparently exist
he used to rock from side to side in bed
Eteocles is still here
if he is dead his legacy continues
what is done in his name
for he does apparently exist
I betrayed my brother

I betrayed my proof
piecing it together

literati

don't tell me I can't repeat myself
I can chant it if I like
put it all in one place
see the pieces fall
all my unfinished sentences
broken shells
topic switch blade
I watch the light on the surface reverberate
off the red wine in the bottle on the table
I was kicked out of family
I can hit but not defend
when a boxing coach says jab
you say
direct from brain to fist
he sees an opening
I betrayed my brother
he betrayed me
I can love but I was not loved
there are many Ismenes internalised many Antigones
I am both all nothing neither
I've told you this before
petals blink in the rain
when my fathers, brothers, uncles
I went away, the same place I go
when I don't finish
my sentences you get frustrated
the wine is not mine neither are you
that's not my sentence
repeat yourself

be the hands that knead
bind
I was asked to hold my hand out for the strap
the training was to hold your hand
out and receive the strap again again
if you pulled away it doubled
this is a finished sentence
I had to train myself not to blink
to go against instinct
programmed to not self-preserve
some Ismenes' brothers did not kill each other
they became grey with skin pigmentation
some Antigones did not die
they went on to have blogs and Instagram
continue to get their life threatened
so I was trained to hold my hand out for the strap not pull back
when I said I'm going out
my father hit me with an open hand
I have metal in my head and heart
and there is no surgery to take away what I hold
so don't review my poetry as hyperbolic
tell me I can't write in the 'I'
the more private the more public
don't shame me with the self-indulgent accusation
the more personal the more universal
don't tell me there are bigger issues
when people said
you are crazy
not this again bring down the government instead
bad things happen to bad people
why can't you let it go
you are bad
you live in the past

bad people make things up about good people
I will pour alcohol onto this hyperbolic illogic burning me alive
what about the internalised government
I say yes I am bad
I made it up
I go where the ends of my sentences are not
the police said don't fight
you might get hurt
you might get killed
after bruising into the furniture
you happy yes I did get bruises
I stop
stopped
my father's hand left five red finger shape welts on my face
don't give me the fridge magnet
you can't love till you love yourself
longed for because of loss
I loved
five welts on my face
no I'm not going out now
don't silence me just because you don't like my story
this is so hard for you you roll your eyes
say being a trauma survivor is a trend
women cashing in
fuck it I'm out
this still happens to children
there were some Ismenes that aged in the poetry scene
directly indirectly poetry speaks
I knew someone who went to jail for five years
she was a single mum on trumped up charges
for exposing the cover ups the police the politicians
were more than complicit were in the rings the rituals
I tried to stop my sister being taken away in a van

it silenced me even to myself
you can't incarcerate a fictional character
I am Ismene in a contemporary setting
asking what it would be like to live on after the Greek tragedy is over
everyone dead or worse not dead
I've survived a state sanctioned incestuous family model
many
paved my path with precedence
laws have been overturned
at my nephew's funeral I hugged a man
I thought was my ex-brother-in-law's gay brother
how good he was there
after being kicked out of family
it was the other brother up on charges
why was he there
looking so well
my sister so broken sparrow
maybe this will perish
the literati will say it's lost its poetic
survivors speak
so five years later he got 14 months
for sitting at family dinners earning trust

taking children home to instruct them in the middle of the night
some Ismenes become Antigones when they are done

What does it mean to require what breaks you
—— Judith Butler

Break on the rocks, breaking and reforming to break again.
Brake. The drama is burning the limits of love. When he
Freudianly texted that he could do with a hit instead of a hug
I knew not to go over. Addiction is when my choice is gone.
Desire or historically harm can activate. Motherless and not
mine marriage and convention do not believe in me. I can only
do the impossible. Everything dripping with continuity, water,
the currawong call, the magpie warble. Everything aches in the
rain, the joints between words and the space between breaths.
I was formed by breaking against those that would break me.
The moments that wake me to love, that I am not a mistake. So
when I am formless and need to reform I need to resist this tidal
pull. Breaking with those that broke me. So tied to the page, the
home page, the sparrows fly above head level, land on chair backs
as I land writing the continuous present. The light aches for
prayer as awareness displaces denial. An angel streaming water
hand to hand as evening is spooned into the back bar. I'm drunk
on too much too soon and the death of not knowing. How do
you communicate something multiple. The clarity of collision,
as soon as you acknowledge what you have you are losing it.
Only the unnamed has the power to exist without boundaries. A
sparrow and me at the long table, its Happy Hour, the bartender
polishes glasses, finally three friends enter chatting oblivious to
the cathedral of echoing.

death

sleep absorbs me as paper towel absorbs water
dream reflects life lived backwards
the moon is pulled smoothed
into edgeless stones
in the throat of the river
dropped into the green ocean swallow
glass bowl
the life force the love force
the life force is so strong it forces me to breath
breathing in I know I am breathing in
breathing out I know I am breathing out
I have the authority to say this
breathing in I know love is being loved
breathing out I let go and allow love being

Lightning Source UK Ltd.
Milton Keynes UK
UKHW011043241121
394475UK00004B/1209

9 781922 571038